THE PLANT PARADOX

A Complete Roadmap to Weight Loss and Improved Health

Published By Nicholas Thompson

@ Sally Tree

The Plant Paradox: A Complete Roadmap

to Weight Loss and Improved Health

All Right RESERVED

ISBN 978-87-975002-7-9

TABLE OF CONTENTS

vegan Cauliflower Curry Soup 1

Mushroom Soup 3

Black, Lemon Chicken Soup 5

Sweet Potato Baked With Garlic And Kale 7

Portobello Pizza 9

Swedish Meatballs 11

Sausage Muffins 15

Plantain Pancakes 17

Cassava Flour Waffles 19

Paradox Crackers 21

Paradox Cappuccino 23

Tops And Bottoms Celery Soup 24

Raw Mushroom Soup 26

Savory Waffles 28

Chocolate Waffles 29

French Style Crepes 31

Fresh Green Thai Curry 33

Awesome Chipotle Bean Stew 37

Vegetable Moussaka 40

Beet-Berry Booster Juice 43

Energizing Green Juice .0. 44

Hearty Grain Bowls 45

Mexican Brown Rice Bowl 47

Asian-Inspired Soba Noodle Bowl: 49

Pan-Fried Fish (Saeng Sun Jun) 51

Soy Honey Glazed Chicken 53

Orange Pumpkin Pancakes 55

Sweet Potato Slices With Fruits 57

High-Protein Apple Pie Smoothie 58

Pumpkin Sourdough Protein Pancakes 60

Lemon Garlic Herb Salmon 63

Guacamole With Jicama Sticks 64

Turmeric Roasted Almonds 65

Dessert Alternatives 66

Berry And Coconut Milk Parfait 66

Dark Chocolate Avocado Mousse: 67

Baked Cinnamon Apples 68

Green Probiotic Smoothie... 69

Lime, Cucumber, And Celery Shake 70

Ginger, Blueberry Smoothie... 71

Matka Smoothie Bowl... 72

Coconut, Avocado, Apple Keto Smoothie 73

Blueberry Power Shake 74

Vanilla Cherry Coconut Smoothie 75

Red Cabbage And Leek Casserole 76

Low Lectin Guacamole 79

Veggie "Pizza" With Cauliflower Crust 81

Grilled Portobello-Pesto Mini "Pizzas" 84

Roast Parmesan-Scented Cauliflower Mash 86

Recipe #21 Lima Beans, Kale, And Turkey..................... 87

Millet Cakes... 90

Baked Artichoke Hearts.. 93

Veggie Curry With Sweet Potato Noodles..................... 95

- Mint Chocolate Chip-Avocado "Ice Cream" 98
- Flour-Free Chocolate-Almond Cake 100
- Orange Chicken With Cranberry Sauce 102
- Loaded Breakfast Muffins 104
- Holiday Muffins 107
- Carrot Bread 110
- Pumpkin Pie... 111
- Spiced Fruit Salad 115
- Vegan Chocolate Mousse.. 117
- Nests Of Sweet Potato Eggs 119
- Tortillas Using Cassava Flour.. 122
- Flapjacks With Cinnamon Cassava Flour 125
- Soy Honey Salmon... 128
- Spicy Pork (Daeji Bulgogi).. 130
- Spicy Rice Cakes (Duk Boki)... 132
- Energizing Daily Tonic 135
- Strawberry Maple Scones 137
- High-Protein Vanilla And Cashew Smoothie 139

Spinach Tofu Scramble With Sour Cream 140

Vegan Cauliflower Curry Soup

Ingredients:

- 1 tbsp Extra-Virgin Olive Oil
- Toasted macadamia nuts, sliced for garnish
- C teaspoon ground cumin
- Sea salt to taste
- ½ head cut cauliflower into bite-sized pieces
- 1 cup full-fat coconut milk
- Sliced Sitaphal for garnish
- 1 teaspoon fresh ginger, finely chopped
- 1 teaspoon curry powder
- 4 cups homemade vegetable broth or chicken broth
- Ch onion, chopped

- 1 garlic clove, minced meat

Direction:

1. Heat extra virgin olive oil in a saucepan. Add in garlic, cauliflower, onion, spices and ginger. Stir the cauliflower until it is brown and the onion is translucent.
2. Then, add vegetable or chicken broth, sea salt and coconut milk. Reduce heat and cook until tender. Blend the mixture, and adjust the spice to your taste.
3. Then, serve the soup and garnish with macadamia nuts, cilantro, and coconut yogurt.

mushroom soup

Ingredients:

- 2 tablespoons chopped red onion
- ¼ cup raw walnuts, or almond butter or hemp seed hearts
- ¼ teaspoon iodized sea salt
-) Spoon Truffle Oil (optional)
- 1/8 teaspoon black pepper cracked.
- 1 fresh oregano sprig
- 1 tablespoon mushroom stem
- ½ cup water

Direction:

1. Cut the mushrooms in half and set aside. Add leftover mushrooms, walnuts, salt, onion, parsley, black pepper and water to the food processor.
2. Pulse ingredients for 25–30 seconds, then mix for 1 minute.
3. Inspect the mixture for temperature, it should be hot. However, if you like it hot, you can

either mix on high for 1 minute or put the ingredients in a saucepan for too long and simmer for a few minutes.
4. Take out of heat and pour the soup into the soup bowl. The texture should be gravy-like and thick.
5. Then, garnish your soup with sliced mushrooms and drizzle with truffle oil.

Black, Lemon Chicken Soup

Ingredients:

- 2 teaspoons extra-virgin olive oil
- Half lemon juice
- Black pepper, fresh ground to taste
- 1 tablespoon fresh lemon juice
- 1 stalk celery, minced or chopped
- 1 bunch bananas, sliced into 1 inch pieces
- Freshly Permigiana Regigo, freshly grated (for service)
- ½ cup cooked chicken, chopped or sliced.
- 3 cloves garlic, minced
- Oon Spoon Balsamic Vinegar
- 3 cups homemade salt free chicken or vegetable stock
- ½ medium onion, finely cooked
- Sea salt to taste
- Oon Spoon Dijon Mustard

Direction:

1. Over medium heat, heat extra-virgin olive oil in a large saucepan (crock-pot or Dutch oven). Pour in garlic, onion, and celery, along with a small pinch of black pepper and sea salt.
2. Pan-fry until the celery is very tender, and the onions become translucent. Pour with cubed or sliced chicken, kale, and djon mustard, lemon zest, and pan-fry for 3-5 minutes.
3. Pour in vegetable or chicken broth, lemon juice and balsamic vinegar, then reduce heat. Cover the pot, warm for 20-25 minutes before serving.

Sweet Potato Baked With Garlic and Kale

Ingredients:

- Sweet potatoes (1 small or medium)
- Olive oil
- Kale (any variety, finely sliced with stems removed), 1 cup
- Sea salt
- 2 crushed garlic cloves

Direction:

1. Peel, wash, and scrub the sweet potato and make a few slices into the top, or poke with a fork.
2. Wrap the potatoes in tin foil and poke with the fork a couple of times. Set oven to 350 degrees, once preheated, add the dish for

approximately 45-60 min or until the sweet potatoes are tender and flaky inside.
3. They can be baked directly in the rack in the oven or a pan. As the sweet potatoes bake, prepare a skillet with one tablespoon of olive oil. Toss in the crushed garlic cloves, sliced kale, and sea salt. Saute on medium until the kale is crispy (or almost crispy). If the kale is done before the sweet potatoes, turn off the stovetop and cover with a lid until they are ready. Serve the sweet potatoes with a drizzle of olive oil and top with the garlic and kale mix to serve.

Portobello Pizza

Ingredients:

- Pepperoni or prosciutto slices
- Olive oil
- Sea salt and black pepper
- Portobello mushroom caps
- Basil pesto, 1-2 teaspoons
- Shredded mozzarella cheese, 1 cup

Direction:

1. If desired, grill or roast the portobello mushroom caps for 2-3 minutes, then top with a drizzle of olive oil, shredded mozzarella cheese, pepperoni or prosciutto slices, basil pesto, and top with black pepper, sea salt

and/or other spices and seasoning, as preferred. Set oven to 350 degrees, once preheated add pizza fr approximately 20 min, until crust is golden and serve.

Swedish Meatballs

Ingredients:

Mustard powder, ½ teaspoon

- White or yellow onion, finely diced, ¼ cup
- Mushrooms, 4 large, diced or minced
- Ground black pepper, ¼ teaspoon
- Parsley, chopped finely, fresh or dried, ¼ cup
- 1 egg
- 1 lb of ground beef
- Sea salt, 1 teaspoon
- Almond flour, 3 teaspoons
- Onion powder, 1 teaspoon

To make the sauce:

- ¼ ground mustard powder

- Garlic powder, 1 tsp

- Sour cream or coconut cream (dairy-free sour cream alternative), ¾ cup

- Parsley, finely chopped or diced, 2 tablespoons

- Sea salt and black pepper to taste

- Fish sauce, 1 teaspoon

- Coconut oil or butter, 1 tablespoon (olive oil can also be used)

- White onion, sliced, ½ cup

- Mushrooms, 4 large, sliced

- Beef broth or stock, 2 cups

- Balsamic vinegar, 1 tsp

Direction:

2. To prepare this recipe, preheat the oven to a temperature of 425 degrees and use a silicone mat or tin foil to line a cookie or baking sheet. Combine the ground beef, mushrooms, minced onions, eggs, parsley, spices, and almond flour in a large bowl.
3. When the ingredients are well mixed, form into balls that are roughly 1-2 inches in diameter.
4. Make sure each of the portions are equal in size, then place on the tray. Bake for approximately 10-12 min, then flip meatballs and continue cooking for 9-10 min, until they are brown and cooked thoroughly. As the meatballs bake, the sauce can be prepared.

5. Over med-hi heat use a large skillet to warm coconut oil or butter, then toss in the mushrooms and onion.

6. Saute these ingredients for 4-5 minutes, the mushrooms and onions should become tender. Pour in the beef stock or broth and stir for a minute, then add in the spices, fish sauce, and balsamic vinegar to cook on medium for another 5 minutes. Place the meatballs into the sauce and cook on low, simmering for about 7-8 minutes or until the sauce is lighter and reduced in volume.

7. Take the skillet off of the burner and stir in the sour cream (or coconut cream), then top with parsley. Add a bit of sea salt and ground black pepper, then serve with salad, noodles, or a side dish of your choice.

Sausage Muffins

Ingredients:

- 1 pound of Turkey Italian Sausage or Turkey Chorizo
- One 10-ounce bag of chopped spinach or kale
- 5 pastured eggs
- 2 tablespoons of Italian seasoning
- 2 tablespoons onion powder
- 1/2 teaspoon of sea salt
- 1/2 teaspoon of cracked pepper
- 2 tablespoons extra-virgin olive oil
- 1 teaspoon of garlic powder
- 2 cloves peeled garlic

Directions:
1. Preheat the oven to 350°F.

2. Line a 6-cup muffin tin using paper liners.
3. Mash the sausage and put in on a frying pan and cook it on medium heat for 10 minutes.
4. Poke small holes in the spinach or kale bag, put in a bowl, and place in the microwave for 3 minutes.
5. Cut an edge off the bag's corner and squeeze the water out.
6. Place all the ingredients but the sausage in a blender and mix for about 1 minute.
7. Put it in a bowl and mix in the cooked sausage.
8. Scoop the mix into the tins and bake for 35 minutes and let it rest a bit before eating.

Plantain Pancakes

Ingredients:

- 2 large green peeled plantains
- 4 large pastured eggs
- 5 tablespoons of coconut oil
- 2 teaspoons of pure vanilla extract
- 1/2 teaspoon baking soda
- 1/4 cup of xylitol
- 1/8 teaspoon of iodized sea salt

Directions:

1. Puree the plantain using a processor or boil them and then smash them.
2. Add the eggs and blend to form a smooth paste.
3. Now you can add the vanilla, half of the coconut oil and the rest of the ingredients until it is smooth.
4. Heat an extra tablespoon of coconut oil in a pan.

5. When hot, use ½ a cup measure and pour batter into the skillet.
6. Cook 5 minutes until the top is dry and has some bubbles, flip it and cook for another 2 minutes.
7. Repeat until you've used the entire mix.

Cassava Flour Waffles

Ingredients:

- 4 eggs
- 1/2 cup cassava flour (or tapioca flour)
- 1/2 cup of melted coconut oil
- 1 tablespoon of honey
- ¼ teaspoon of salt
- 1/2 teaspoon baking soda
- 1 package of frozen unsweetened wild blueberries

Directions:
1. Preheat a waffle iron.
2. Then, add the eggs, the flour, oil, baking soda, salt and honey (or sugar) to a blender and mix them until you have a smooth mix.
3. Using a 1/4 cup measure, scoop mix into the waffle iron and cook.

4. Then you can add some more honey and the blueberries.

Paradox Crackers

Ingredients:

- 2 large pastured eggs
- 1 teaspoon of filtered water
- 1 cup of almond flour
- 1/2 cup coconut flour
- 1 teaspoon of your preferred seasoning
- 1/2 teaspoon of salt

Directions:

1. Preheat your oven to 350°F.
2. Whisk the eggs and water in a bowl.
3. In another bowl mix both flours, the salt, and the seasoning.
4. Add the egg and blend with a spatula until you eliminate any lumps.
5. Form small marble-sized balls and put them on a cookie sheet.

6. Press them with a fork and bake for 20 minutes.

Paradox Cappuccino

Ingredients:

- 1 cup hot coffee
- 1 tablespoon MCT oil
- 1 tablespoon of grass-fed butter or goat butter
- 1 pack of stevia

Directions:

1. Place the ingredients in a mixer for 30 seconds.
2. Put it into a mug and serve your cappuccino.
3. That's it!

Tops and Bottoms Celery Soup

Ingredients:

- 3 tablespoons of olive oil (avocado oil also works)
- 1-pound of peeled and cut celery root
- 2 celery stems with leaves, cut into small pieces
- 1/2 of chopped red onion
- 1 tablespoon of chopped rosemary leaves
- 1/2 teaspoon sea salt
- 1/2 teaspoon black pepper
- 3 cups of vegetable broth
- 1/2 lemon juice

Directions:

1. In a heavy saucepan on medium heat, heat the 3 tablespoons of olive oil, and then add

chopped celery root, celery leaves, onion, rosemary and salt, and pepper.
2. Cook for 5 minutes until de celery roots start to soften.
3. Now you can add the broth and lemon until it boils.
4. At this point reduce the heat, cover the mix and let it simmer for half an hour.
5. Stir once in a while and check if the celery root is soft.
6. Once it is tender, remove the soup from the stove.
7. Pass half of the soup to a blender and blend it until it's creamy.
8. Repeat with the rest and reheat the whole soup in the saucepan for another 5 minutes.
9. You're good to serve.

Raw Mushroom Soup

Ingredients:

1. 2 ½ cups of your preferred mushrooms
2. 1/2 cup almond butter
3. 1 tablespoon dried onion or 3 tablespoons of sliced red onion
4. 1/2 teaspoon of sea salt
5. 1/4 teaspoon of black pepper
6. 2 fresh thyme leaves
7. 1 tablespoon truffle oil

Directions:

1. Cut 1/2 cup of the mushrooms and set aside.
2. Then, put the other 2 cups of mushrooms, the water, almond butter, onions, salt, pepper, and thyme in a food processor.
3. Process high for 30 seconds, and then blend for 2 minutes.
4. Check the temperature as it should be just warm.

5. If you want it to be hotter you can blend for another minute.
6. The texture should be somewhat gravy-like.
7. Serve in a bowl and top with the rest of the diced mushrooms and sprinkle with the truffle oil.

Savory Waffles

Ingredients:

- 1 medium sweet potato, peeled, grated and squeezed
- Salt to taste
- 1/2 teaspoon dried rosemary, crushed
- 1/8 teaspoon red pepper flakes, crushed

Directions:

1. Preheat the waffle iron and grease it.
2. In a bowl, add ingredients and mix well.
3. Add half of the mixture in preheated waffle iron and cook for 10 minutes.
4. Repeat with the remaining mixture.
5. Serve warm.

Chocolate Waffles

Ingredients:

For Waffles:

- ¼ cup 70% dark chocolate chips
- 1 cup blanched almond flour
- ¼ cup cacao powder
- ¼ cup coconut flour
- ½ teaspoon baking soda
- ½ teaspoon organic vanilla extract

For Sauce:

- 2 tablespoons coconut oil
- ¼ cup 70% dark chocolate chips

Directions:

1. Preheat the waffle iron and grease it.
2. In a mixing bowl, mix together cocoa powder, baking soda, flours, and salt.

3. In another bowl, add honey, vanilla extract and eggs mix well.
4. Add the egg mixture into bowl with flour mixture and mix well.
5. Gently, fold in chocolate chips.
6. Add ¾ cup of mixture to waffle iron. Cook for 5 minutes.
7. Repeat with remaining mixture.
8. For the sauce, in a small pan, add coconut oil and chocolate chips over low heat and melt while stirring continuously.
9. Serve the waffles with the topping of chocolate sauce.

French Style Crepes

Ingredients:

- 2 tablespoons arrowroot powder
- 1 tablespoon olive oil
- 1 teaspoon organic vanilla extract
- Salt to taste
- 4 organic eggs
- ½ teaspoon ground cinnamon
- 2 tablespoons almond flour

Directions:
1. In a mixing bowl, add almond flour, arrowroot powder, salt and cinnamon and mix well.
2. In another bowl, add vanilla and eggs and beat until well combined.
3. Add the egg mixture into flour mixture and mix well.

4. Using a non-stick pan heat the oil over medium heat.
5. Add the desired amount of mixture to pan to coat the bottom in a thin layer.
6. Cook for 1 minute per side.
7. Repeat with the remaining mixture.

Fresh Green Thai Curry

Ingredients:

Curry Paste

- 4 stalks of lemon grass (outer peel removed before chopping finely)

- Good thumb size piece of fresh ginger peeled and grated

- 6 green chilies de-seeded and chopped

- Rind and juice of 1 lime and 1 small lemon

- Large bunch of cilantros washed and chopped (including stalks)

- 2 tablespoons soy sauce

- 1 x 13.5 fluid oz can of organic unsweetened coconut milk (full fat)

Curry

- 2 cups of chick peas cooked and rinsed
- 2 cups green peas or snow peas
- 2 cups (packed) kale, chopped with stalk removed
- 10 fine fresh asparagus spears cut into 2-inch pieces
- 2 cups Thai rice
- Black pepper

Garnish

- Some of the cilantro leaves reserved
- 1 lime cut into quarters

Directions:

1. To make the curry paste, add all the ingredients except the coconut milk and soy

sauce, to a blender or food processor and blend until they form a paste.
2. Add the coconut milk to the paste and blend again until fully combined.
3. Finally, add the soy sauce and mix it in.
4. Cook the rice following the manufacturer's guidelines, when it is cooked drain and rinse it thoroughly in cold water, drain again and set aside.
5. Meanwhile in a skillet put the chickpeas and curry sauce you have just made, season with some freshly ground black pepper and cook covered on a low heat for 15 minutes.
6. Add the kale and peas and cook covered for a further 5 minutes or until the kale has wilted.
7. While the curry is cooking, fry the asparagus gently until golden.
8. Boil a kettle full of water.
9. Add the asparagus to the curry remove from the heat and keep covered.

10. Pour the boiling water all over the rice, allowing the water to drain, then immediately plate it up.
11. Put the curry on top of the rice and sprinkle a little of the reserved cilantro on top to garnish.
12. Add a wedge of lime to the plate and serve immediately.
13. You can prepare the curry paste including the coconut milk and soy sauce ahead of time and refrigerate it in an airtight container for up to 5 days or freeze for up to 2 months.

Awesome Chipotle Bean Stew

Ingredients:

Veg

- 4 cups of waxy potatoes cut up into large chunks
- 1 1/s cups of dry pinto beans (or similar)
- 2 cups of carrots cut up into chunks
- 1 cup celery cut up into chunks
- 2 cups of bell peppers cut up into chunks
- 2 cups firm tomatoes cut up into chunks
- 1 large yellow onion diced
- 3 cups kale, bok choy or dark green cabbage to add in the final 30 minutes of cooking
- Unsalted cooked cashews, added once the stew is cooked

Broth

- 2 cups of water

- 6 cups vegetable broth, homemade or low sodium shop brought (this needs to be sufficient to cover all the vegetables when ingredients are placed into the slow cooker).

- 2 – 4 tablespoons arrowroot powder

- 4 garlic segments mashed

- 2 tablespoons chipotle chili spice

- 1 tablespoon garlic powder

- 1 tablespoon onion powder

- Freshly ground black pepper to taste

- Salt to taste

Directions:

1. Put the vegetable broth and water into a slow cooker (note that sodium will make the beans tough, so try to use low sodium broth).

2. Add the prepared veg except the greens and cashews. There should be about an inch of liquid covering the vegetables, add more broth if required.
3. Cook on high for 5 to 6 hours or on low at 8 to 9 hours.
4. In the final half hour of cooking put the arrowroot powder, garlic, chipotle, garlic powder and onion powder with a ¼ cup of water.
5. Blend on high speed until smooth (add more liquid if required). Add this to the broth in the slow cooker and whisk it in until well combined.
6. Chop the greens (removing any coarse stalks) and add to the stew allow to wilt.
7. Finally, add the cashew nuts and stir well.
8. Serve immediately.

Vegetable Moussaka

Ingredients:

- 5 tablespoons vegetable oil
- 1 large eggplant cut into thin slices
- 1 large onion chopped
- 4 ounces mushrooms sliced
- 2 garlic cloves crushed
- 4 tomatoes, skins removed (soak in boiling water for 5 minutes) and chopped
- 1 tablespoon of tomato puree
- 2 tablespoons apple cider vinegar
- 1 tablespoon mixed herbs
- 3 ounces of walnuts, chopped
- 1-ounce whole meal breadcrumbs
- Salt and pepper to taste

- 1-ounce whole meal flour

- ½ pint almond milk

- Extra walnuts to garnish

Directions:

1. Pre-heat the oven to 350 degrees Fahrenheit
2. In a skillet heat 2 tablespoons of oil and fry the eggplant on both sides, drain on kitchen paper and set aside.
3. Add another 1 tablespoon of oil to the pan and sauté the chopped onion until cooked through.
4. Add the mushrooms and garlic to the pan and cook for a further 5 minutes on a medium heat.
5. Add the tomatoes, tomato puree, vinegar and herbs and cook on a low heat until it forms a sauce.
6. Add the walnuts, breadcrumbs, salt and pepper, add a drop more oil if necessary.

7. In a saucepan, make the white sauce by adding any remaining oil, flour and almond milk, whisk continually for around 5 minutes over a very gentle heat until it has become smooth and thick.
8. Lightly grease a shallow ovenproof dish. Place some of the eggplant slices next to one another on the base.
9. Spoon half of the nut mixture into the dish and cover with half of the white sauce.
10. Place the remaining eggplant slices on top and add another layer of nut mixture and white sauce.
11. Bake in the oven for 30 minutes. Halfway through cooking time you can add the extra nuts.
12. Serve with a side of salad or potatoes and vegetables as desired.

Beet-Berry Booster Juice

Ingredients:

- 1 small beet, peeled and chopped
- 1 cup of mixed berries (strawberries, raspberries, blackberries)
- 1 cup of coconut water or plant-based milk (almond or soy) 1 tablespoon of chia seeds
- Optional: a squeeze of lemon juice or a teaspoon of honey for sweetness

Directions:

1. Place the chopped beet, mixed berri es, coconut water or plant-based milk, chia seeds, and optional lemon juice or honey in a blender.
2. Blend until all the ingredients are well combined and the juice is smooth.
3. Pour into a glass and enjoy this vibrant and nutrient
4. juice, packed with antioxidants, fiber, and natural sweetness.

Energizing Green Juice .0.

Ingredients:

- 2 green apples, cored and chopped
- 2 large celery stalks
- 1 cucumber
- 1 small handful of spinach or kale
- 1-inch piece of ginger
- Optional: a squeeze of lemon juice for a tangy kick

Directions:

Run the green apples, celery stalks, cucumber, spinach or kale, and ginger through a juicer.

Stir in the optional lemon juice to add a tangy flavor.

Pour the juice into a glass and enjoy this invigorating green juice, packed with vitamins, mine rals, and detoxifying properties.

Hearty Grain Bowls

Ingredients:

- 1 cup cooked quinoa
- ½ cup cherry tomatoes, halved
- ½ cucumber, diced
- ½ cup kalamata olives, pitted and sliced ¼ red onion, thinly sliced
- ¼ cup crumbled feta cheese (optional)
- Fresh parsley or basil, chopped
- Lemon wedges for serving

Directions:

1. In a bowl, combine the cooked quinoa, cherry tomatoes, cucumber, kalamata olives, red onion, and optional feta cheese.
2. Toss the ingredients together and sprinkle with fresh parsley or basil.

3. Squeeze lemon juice over the bowl before serving.
4. If desired, add grilled tofu or ch ickpeas for additional protein.
5. Enjoy this Mediterranean-inspired grain bowl that is packed with fresh flavors and wholesome ingredients.

Mexican Brown Rice Bowl

Ingredients:

- 1 cup cooked brown rice
- ½ cup black beans, rinsed and drained
- ½ cup corn kernels
- ½ bell pepper, diced
- ¼ red onion, diced
- ½ avocado, sliced
- Fresh cilantro, chopped
- Lime wedges for serving

Directions:

1. In a bowl, combine the cooked brown rice, black beans, corn kernels, bell pepper, red onion, and sliced avocado.
2. Mix the ingredients together and sprinkle with fresh cilantro.

3. Squeeze lime juice over the bowl before serving.
4. If desired, add a dollop of salsa, Greek yogurt, or vegan sour cream for extra flavor and creaminess.
5. Enjoy this Mexican-inspired grain bowl that is packed with vibrant colors, textures, and a touch of zesty goodness.

Asian-Inspired Soba Noodle Bowl:

Ingredients:

- 2 ounces of soba noodles, cooked according to package instructions
- ½ cup edamame beans, cooked and shelled ½ cup shredded carrots
- ½ cup sliced cucumber
- ¼ cup sliced scallions
- ¼ cup chopped peanuts or cashews
- Fresh cilantro or Thai basil, chopped

Directions:

1. In a bowl, combine the cooked soba noodles, edamame beans, shredded carrots, sliced cucumber, and sliced scallions.
2. Toss the ingredients together and sprinkle with chopped peanuts or cashews.
3. Garnish with fresh cilantro or Thai basil.

4. If desired, add cooked tofu or tempeh for additional protein.
5. Enjoy this Asian -inspired grain bowl that is full of vibrant flavors, crunchy textures, and a touch of nuttiness.

Pan-Fried Fish (saeng sun jun)

Ingredients:

- 16oz [450g] White Fish, or Vegan Fish (fillets)
- 3 Tbsp [45mL] Cassava, Tapioca, Sorghum, or Almond Flour
- 2 Eggs
- ¼ cup [120mL] Avocado or Coconut Oil
- 1 Tbsp [15mL] Iodized Sea Salt (plus more to taste)
- 1 tsp [5mL] Black Pepper

Directions:

1. Cut the fillets diagonally, with the grain, so the pieces are about 1 ½" [3cm] thick.
2. Salt and pepper the fish, or vegan fish on both sides.

3. In a small mixing bowl, beat the eggs with a pinch of salt.
4. Add the flour into a dish next to the eggs.
5. In a medium pan, add the oil and set it on medium-high heat.
6. Dip each fish, or vegan fish piece in flour, then egg to coat it thoroughly. Then place them in the hot pan.
7. Fry the fish, or vegan fish, for 2-3 minutes on each side. Be mindful to not overcook the fish or it will dry out
8. Remove the fish from the pan and let it drain. Serve hot, and add extra salt if needed. Eat as is, or serve with coconut aminos, spicy dipping sauce, or gochujang sauce.

Soy Honey Glazed Chicken

Ingredients:

- 32oz [900g] chicken, vegan meat, or veggies (cubed or in strips)
- ½ cup [120mL] Coconut Aminos
- ½ cup [120g] Swerve (or sweetener substitute)
- ½ cup [120mL] Olive Oil (or avocado, or perilla oil)
- 1 tsp [5mL] Iodized Sea Salt

Directions:

1. In a large bowl, add the coconut aminos, swerve, olive oil and salt. Whisk or mix vigorously with a fork. Alternatively, use a hand mixer, or blend.

2. In a pan, add the chicken/vegan meat and the blended sauce. Cook on medium-high until the sauce caramelizes, about 20 minutes, stirring at the 10-minute mark and as the sauce thickens.
3. Serve, and enjoy!

ORANGE PUMPKIN PANCAKES

Ingredients:

- 10 g ground flax meal
- 45 ml water
- 235 ml unsweetened soy milk
- 15 ml lemon juice
- 60 g buckwheat flour
- 60 g all-purpose flour
- 8 g baking powder, aluminum-free
- 2 tsp finely grated orange zest
- 25 g white chia seeds
- 120 g organic pumpkin puree (or just bake the pumpkin and puree the flesh)
- 30 ml melted and cooled coconut oil
- 5 ml vanilla paste

- 30 ml pure maple syrup

Directions:

1. Combine ground flax meal with water in a small bowl. Place aside for 10 minutes. Combine almond milk and cider vinegar in a medium bowl. Place aside for 5 minutes.
2. In a separate large bowl, combine buckwheat flour, all-purpose flour, baking powder, orange zest, and chia seeds.
3. Pour in almond milk, along with pumpkin puree, coconut oil, vanilla, and maple syrup.
4. Whisk together until you have a smooth batter.
5. Heat large non-stick skillet over medium-high heat. Brush the skillet gently with some coconut oil.
6. Pour 60ml of batter into skillet. Cook the pancake for 1 minute, or until bubbles appear on the surface.

SWEET POTATO SLICES WITH FRUITS

Ingredients:

- 1 sweet potato Topping.
- 60 g organic peanut butter.
- 30ml pure maple syrup.
- 4 dried apricots, sliced.
- 30 g fresh raspberries.

Directions:

1. Peel and cut sweet potato into 1/2 cm thick slices.
2. Place the potato slices in a toaster on high for 5 minutes. Toast your sweet potatoes TWICE.
3. Arrange sweet potato slices onto a plate.
4. Spread the peanut butter over sweet potato slices.
5. Drizzle the maple syrup over the butter. Top each slice with an equal amount of sliced apricots and raspberries. Serve.

HIGH-PROTEIN APPLE PIE SMOOTHIE

Ingredients:

- 1 cup of almond milk.
- 1 scoop plant-based vanilla protein powder.
- 1/4 cup gluten-free rolled oats.
- 1 medium apple, peeled, cored and sliced.
- 1/2 frozen banana.
- 1/2 tsp vanilla extract.
- 1 tsp maple syrup.
- 1 tsp cinnamon.
- Pinch nutmeg.
- Pinch ground ginger.
- Ice, as needed.

Direction:

1. Add all active ingredients to a high speed mixer.

2. Mix on high till smooth.
3. Add ice into a mixer if you need a cold smoothie.
4. Pour into a glass and take pleasure in.

PUMPKIN SOURDOUGH PROTEIN PANCAKES

Ingredients:

Overnight sponge:

- 1/4 cup gluten-free sourdough starter.

- 1/4 cup pumpkin puree.

- 1/2 cup chickpea flour (or any other gluten-free flour).

- 1/2 cup almond milk.

- 1-2 tbsp maple syrup.

In the morning:

- 1 flax egg (1 tbsp ground flaxseed + 3 tbsp water).

- 1 tsp pumpkin spice.

- 1 tsp cinnamon.

- 1/2 tsp turmeric.

- 1/4 cup raw cacao nibs (or non-diary chocolate chips).

- A handful of sliced pecans (optional however extremely advised!).

- 1/2 tsp baking soda.

- 1 tsp baking powder.

Direction:

1. The night before making the pancakes, position the overnight sponge ingredients into a non-reactive bowl. Mix well, cover with plastic wrap and let it sit overnight.
2. In the morning, before you make the pancakes, add all the other ingredients (other than baking powder and baking soda) into the overnight sponge. Stir well.
3. Heat a non-stick pan over medium heat.
4. Add baking soda and baking powder to the batter and carefully stir them in.

5. Put 1/4 cup of the batter onto the pan for each pancake and fry until you see bubbles forming on the surface area of the pancakes and the edges dry out.

Lemon Garlic Herb Salmon

Ingredients*:*

- Wild-caught salmon fillet
- Lemon juice, garlic, and fresh herbs for marinade
- Roasted Brussels sprouts for side

Direction:

1. Marinate salmon in a mixture of lemon juice, minced garlic, and fresh herbs.
2. Roast Brussels sprouts and serve alongside the lemon garlic herb salmon.

Guacamole with Jicama Sticks

Ingredients:

- Avocado, mashed
- Diced tomatoes, onions, cilantro
- Lime juice
- Jicama sticks for dipping

Direction:

1. Prepare guacamole by mixing mashed avocado, diced tomatoes, onions, cilantro, and lime juice.
2. Enjoy with jicama sticks for a refreshing and crunchy snack.

Turmeric Roasted Almonds

Ingredients:

- Almonds
- Olive oil
- Turmeric, salt, and pepper

Direction:

1. Toss almonds with olive oil, turmeric, salt, and pepper.
2. Roast until golden brown for a flavorful and anti-inflammatory snack.

Dessert Alternatives

Berry and Coconut Milk Parfait

Ingredients:

- Mixed berries
- Coconut milk
- Shredded coconut for topping

Direction:

1. Layer mixed berries with coconut milk in a glass.
2. Top with shredded coconut for a simple and satisfying dessert.

Dark Chocolate Avocado Mousse:

**Ingredients*:*

- Ripe avocado

- Dark chocolate (70% cocoa or higher)

- Maple syrup for sweetness

Direction:

1. Blend ripe avocado, melted dark chocolate, and maple syrup until smooth.
2. Chill before serving for a creamy and indulgent mousse.

Baked Cinnamon Apples

Ingredients:

- Apple, cored and sliced
- Cinnamon
- Coconut oil

**Direction*:*

1. Toss apple slices with cinnamon and a touch of melted coconut oil.
2. Bake until tender for a warm and comforting dessert.

Green Probiotic Smoothie

Ingredients:

- Ha Kombucha Tea
- 1 teaspoon chia seeds
- 1 fist baby spinach
- 1 teaspoon grass fed collagen
- ¼ cup frozen mixed berries
- ¼ avocado, peeled and pitted
- ¼ cup coconut milk

Direction:

1. In a food processor mix all the ingredients together with a discount for chia seeds. After the ingredients are blended until smooth.
2. Then add in chia seeds, do some quick pulse to mix well.

Lime, Cucumber, and Celery Shake

Ingredients:

- ½ small cucumbers, sliced, peeled, sliced and deseeded.
- Ice lime juice
- Ice cup ice
- ¼ cup of water
- 2 stalks and bite-sized portion of celery heart
- 1 alcohol pill (optional)

Direction:

1. Put everything in a food processor and mix easily. Strain the smoothie to get the juice. Serve with two to three cubes of ice.

Ginger, Blueberry Smoothie

Ingredients:

- 12 blueberries
- Ut Cup Coconut Yogurt
- ½ cup 240 ml coconut milk mixed
- 2 slices ginger
- 1 slice apple
- Stevia to taste
- CT Spoon MCT Oil
- ¼ tbsp collagen powder

Direction:

1. Add all ingredients to a food processor and mix until smooth.

Matka Smoothie Bowl

Ingredients:

- Ch Tbsp Chia Seeds
- Oon Spoon Matka Powder
- 6 oz Coconut Yoghurt or Greek Yoghurt
- 1 teaspoon greens powder (optional)
- Stevia to taste
- ½ teaspoon goji berries
- 1 teaspoon coconut flakes
- C Tbsp cacao nibs

Direction:

1. Add the curd to the matka and mix. If you wish, add it to stevia to make it sweeter. Empty the mixed smoothie in a bowl. Garnish with cacao nib, chia seeds, coconut flakes and goji berries.

Coconut, Avocado, Apple Keto Smoothie

Ingredients:

- 1 medium avocado, rinsed, peeled, and destined
- CT Spoon MCT Oil
- 1 apple slice
- ½ tbsp collagen powder
- 1 teaspoon lemon juice
- ¼ cup non-milk coconut milk
- ½ teaspoon chopped uncooked coconut for garnish

Direction:

1. **Combine all ingredients in a food processor and mix until smooth. Top with sliced coconut.**

Blueberry Power Shake

**Ingredients*:*

- ½ cup coconut milk
- 4 snowflakes
- ¼ cup Greek yogurt or plain yogurt
- ¼ cup fresh or frozen blueberries or blueberries
- Eas Spoon Pure Vanilla Extracts
- ½ tbsp virgin coconut oil
- Stevia to taste or any dessert you like.

Direction:

1. Add all ingredients to a food processor. Blend until smooth until frozen or ice fruit is mixed. Adjust sweetness if necessary. service tax.

Vanilla Cherry Coconut Smoothie

Ingredients:

- 2 ounces frozen sweet cherries
- 2 ounces of water
- 2 ounces full-fat canned coconut milk
- ¾ teaspoon pure vanilla powder
- 4 to 6 snowflakes
- A pinch of sea salt, finely ground

Direction:

1. Add all the components in a food processor, mixing until smooth. Add some ice cubes and serve.

Red Cabbage and Leek Casserole

Ingredients:

- Large or medium head of cabbage (red or green cabbage)
- 2 medium-sized leeks, washed and sliced (green onions can be used if leeks are not available)
- Sea salt and ground black pepper to taste
- Fennel seeds, ½ teaspoon
- Fresh or dried dill, 1 teaspoon of dried, or a small handful of fresh and finely diced
- Olive oil for cooking, extra virgin oil is recommended

Direction:

1. To prepare the cabbage, shred with a large grater by hand and into a large bowl. The amount of cabbage may appear excessive at first, though once cooked, it will reduce in size.
2. Prepare the oven by preheating to a temperature of 400 degrees. Slice the leeks finely and add them to the cabbage to distribute and blend evenly.
3. Add in the fennel seeds, dill, ground black pepper, and sea salt to mix. Line a casserole dish with parchment paper and lightly sprinkle with oil.
4. Once the ingredients in the bowl are well mixed, pour them into the casserole dish and drizzle the olive oil evenly over the ingredients.
5. Place the casserole dish into the oven to bake for 15 minutes on the middle rack of the oven.

6. If the vegetables are not softened enough, you may bake for another 15-20 minutes. Serve immediately as the main dish, or as a tasty side.

7. There are many variations to this dish, including adding sliced kale, shredded cauliflower or broccoli florets, and onions, if desired. This is a dish that is experimented with and changed at your leisure, with a variety of vegetable blends and flavors.

8. Additional spices, such as chili powder, paprika, cumin, and many others, are also welcome to this dish and can a unique and satisfying twist to the flavor as well.

Low Lectin Guacamole

Ingredients:

2 large avocados, raw and ripe enough to mash and mix

- ½ red onion or 1 small red onion, diced finely
- 2 teaspoons of olive oil
- 3-4 sprigs of cilantro and/or parsley
- black pepper, 1 tsp (fresh ground)
- Seasalt as desired
- Chili pepper, as desired (optional)

Direction:

- Mash the avocados in a large bowl, then stir in the oil, sea salt, chili pepper, and black pepper.

- Mix well, then add in the diced onions and continue to mix.
- Parsley and/or cilantro can be finely diced to add into the recipe or added as a topping or garnish instead.

Veggie "Pizza" with Cauliflower Crust

Ingredients:

- For the Crust:
- Olive oil
- 1 small head cauliflower, riced
- 1 lightly beaten egg
- 1/2 cup of shredded buffalo mozzarella
- 1/2 teaspoon of sea salt,
- 1/2 teaspoon of black pepper
- 1/2 teaspoon of oregano
- **For the Topping**
- Preferred veggies
- 1 cup of grated Pecorino cheese
  Sea salt

Directions:

1. First of all, rice the cauliflower with the biggest part of a cheese grater. You'll end up with about 3 cups.
2. Pass it to a dish and microwave on high for 8 minutes, until it's cooked. Allow to cool, stirring occasionally.
3. Preheat oven to 450°F.
4. Grease an ovenproof frying pan with the olive oil.
5. After the riced cauliflower has cooled down, place it in a dishtowel, and remove all the liquid.
6. Pass it to a bowl and add the rest of the crust ingredients and mix them well.
7. Press the mixture all over the frying pan on the top of the stove and crisp the crust for a couple minutes.
8. Then put in the oven for 15 minutes or until it's golden.

9. Let it cool for a few minutes and add the topping.
10. First, distribute the mozzarella evenly over the crust and add the vegetables of your liking.
11. Scatter the pecorino cheese and add a dash of salt.
12. Bake until the cheese melts, which should be around 10 minutes.

Grilled Portobello-Pesto Mini "Pizzas"

Ingredients:

For the Pesto

- **1 cup of fresh basil leaves**
- **1/4 cup of olive oil**
- **1/2 cup of pine nuts**
- **Two 1-inch chops of Parmigiano Reggiano**

For the Pizzas

- 2 large Portobello mushrooms, stems removed
- Coconut or olive oil
- 2 slices of prosciutto
- 1 ball of chopped buffalo mozzarella
- Sea salt to taste
- Black pepper to taste

Directions:

1. To make the pesto just put all the ingredients in a processor or blender and blend them until they are homogeneous.
2. For the pizzas just place a grill pan on the stove over medium to high heat.
3. Rub the cap of the mushrooms with the oil and place them on the grill with the cap side up for 5 minutes, flip them, and grill them for another 5 minutes and remove.
4. Add 3 tablespoons of pesto over one mushroom, add a slice of prosciutto and top with mozzarella.
5. Return them to the grill and close the hood. Cook until the cheese melts.

Roast Parmesan-Scented Cauliflower Mash

.

Ingredients:

- 1 large head of cut cauliflower
- 1/4 cup olive oil
- Sea salt,
- Cracked black pepper
- 2 tablespoons unsalted of goat butter
- 1 cup of grated Parmigiano Reggiano cheese

Directions:

1. Preheat the oven to 400°F.
2. Then, put the cauliflower flowerets in a bowl.
3. Add the extra virgin olive oil, salt and pepper to taste, and combine.
4. Put a sheet of aluminum foil over the countertop. Fold in half and reopen it.

5. Put the cauliflower in the middle of one half of it. Fold the other half and tuck the edges to seal it.
6. Place on a cookie tray and put it on the middle holder of the oven.
7. Cook until it's tender, which should be about 1 hour and remove.
8. Open the sack without letting the juice go away and let it cool for 10 minutes.
9. Pass it all to a blender.
10. Add the butter and the cheese and season it with salt and pepper.
11. Blend until it's smooth and thick.

Recipe #21 Lima Beans, Kale, and Turkey

Ingredients:

- 1 bunch of black kale

- 1 medium chopped onion

- 2 minced garlic cloves garlic
- 2 tablespoons of olive oil
- 1 pound of dried large lima beans
- 2 teaspoons of Italian seasoning
- 1 small bone-in turkey thigh (3/4 pounds)
- 2 tablespoons of mustard
- Sea salt to taste
- Cracked black pepper to taste

Directions:
1. Cut the leaves off the twigs of the kale.
2. Chop the stems and leaves into large pieces and reserve.
3. Pan-fry the onions and garlic in olive oil for about 5 minutes over medium heat.
4. Pass them to the pressure cooker.
5. Add some veggie stock and water.

6. Then, add the beans, seasoning and the turkey thigh.
7. Cook them all at high pressure for 15 minutes and allow the pressure to come down.
8. Put the turkey aside and shred it.
9. Blend in the kale leaves, mustard and season with salt and pepper.
10. Add the turkey again.
11. Stir it all until it's blended and you're good to go.

Millet Cakes

Ingredients:

- 1/2 cup of millet
- 2 cups of vegetable stock or water
- ¾ teaspoon of sea salt
- 1/4 cup of chopped carrots
- 1/4 cup of chopped basil
- 1/4 cup chopped onion
- 1 cup of chopped mushrooms
- 1 chopped garlic clove
- 1/2 teaspoon Italian seasoning
- 2 tablespoons extra-virgin olive oil
- 1 beaten pastured egg
- 1 tablespoon of coconut flour

Directions:

1. In a saucepan, toast the millet on medium heat for 5 minutes, shaking often, until golden and aromatic.
2. After that, slowly add the vegetable stock and salt.
3. Blend and bring to boiling point.
4. Reduce the heat to seethe, cover the saucepan, and cook for another 15 minutes until the water has been absorbed.
5. Remove from the heat and let it stand covered for 10 minutes, then shake it with a fork.
6. Place the onion, carrots, basil, mushrooms, garlic, and Italian seasoning in a processor and pulse into small pieces.
7. Place 1 tablespoon of the oil in a pan over medium heat and add the vegetable mixture.
8. Fry it 3 or 4 minutes, until it's tender.
9. Pass to a large bowl.

10. Now put the millet, beaten egg, and coconut flour to the bowl and stir them all to mix and thicken.
11. Grease your hands and form 2-inch balls from the mixture and press them to form patties.
12. It should be good to make 12 cakes.
13. Add 1 tablespoon of olive oil to the skillet and sauté the patties over medium heat, 5 minutes each side.

Baked Artichoke Hearts

Ingredients:

- 4 tablespoons of extra-virgin olive oil
- The juice of ½ a lemon
- A pinch of powdered cayenne pepper
- 10 of defrosted frozen artichoke hearts.
- 1 cup of cassava flour
- 1/4 teaspoon of iodized sea salt
- 1/4 teaspoon cracked black pepper
- Lemon slices

Directions:

1. Preheat the oven to 400°F.
2. Add to a mixing bowl 3 tablespoons of the olive oil, lemon juice, and a pinch of cayenne pepper and beat until blended.

3. Now, put the artichoke hearts there and mix them until they are well coated.
4. Grab a rimmed baking sheet and coat it with olive oil.
5. Put the flour, the sea salt, and the pepper in a re-sealable plastic bag and add the artichokes to the bag.
6. Shake them until they are covered.
7. Place the hearts on the sheet and bake them for 25 minutes, shaking the pan a couple of times.
8. Remove to a serving dish and sprinkle with a bit of salt and lemon juice if you like.

Veggie Curry with Sweet Potato Noodles

Ingredients:

For the Curry:

- 1/2 tablespoon of coconut oil
- 1 large carrot, julienne cut
- 1 cup of bite-sized broccoli
- 1/2 cup of chopped onion,
- 1 teaspoon of crushed fresh ginger
- 1 tablespoon of yellow curry powder
- One 13.5-ounce coconut cream
- Pinch sea salt, preferably iodized

For the Noodles:

- 1/2 tablespoon of coconut oil
- 1 large sweet potato, spiralized

- Pinch of salt

Directions:
1. Heat the coconut oil on medium-high heat and add the carrot.
2. Cook it until it starts to become tender, about three minutes.
3. Put the heat down to medium and add the ginger, onions, and broccoli.
4. Cook until they soften, about five minutes.
5. Add the curry and cook for an extra minute.
6. Pour the coconut milk and a pinch of salt and raise the heat to medium-high until it boils.
7. After that, turn it down to medium-low and let it simmer, stirring here and there, for 15 minutes, when it should start to condense.
8. While it's simmering, heat some coconut oil in a frying pan and add the sweet potato noodles.

9. Season with salt and stir them frequently until they start to soften, around 10 minutes.
10. Pass it to the curry pan and mix for about a minute or two before serving.

Mint Chocolate Chip-Avocado "Ice Cream"

Ingredients:

- A 15-ounce can of coconut milk

- 1/3 cup of Swerve, a sweetener

- 1 teaspoon of ground espresso beans

- 2 tablespoons of unsweetened cocoa powder

- 1 bar of diced 85% to 90% sugar-free dark chocolate,

- 1 teaspoon of pure vanilla extract

- 2 Hass avocados

- 3 tablespoons of chopped fresh mint

- 1/2 cup 70% or more sugar-free extra-dark chocolate chips

Directions:

1. Place the milk, Swerve, coffee powder cocoa powder in a medium-sized pan.
2. Blend over medium heat until the powders are dissolved, and the mix has blended.
3. Turn off and add the diced chocolate bar. Stir until it's melted.
4. Put the mix in a food processor and add the vanilla, avocados, and mint.
5. Process until it's smooth.
6. Put into a bowl and cool for 2 hours.
7. Get it out and disperse the chocolate chips.
8. Put the mix into an ice cream maker and mix until it has the consistency of a soft ice cream.
9. Serve.

Flour-free Chocolate-Almond Cake

Ingredients:

1. 2 tablespoons of unsweetened cocoa powder
2. 2 tablespoons of Swerve, a sweetener
3. 1/4 teaspoon of baking powder
4. 1 large egg
5. 1 tablespoon heavy cream
6. 1/2 teaspoon pure vanilla extract
7. 1 teaspoon of salted goat butter
8. 1 tablespoon of almond butter

Directions:

1. Put the cocoa powder, Swerve, and baking powder in a bowl.
2. Whisk with a fork to mix the elements and mash any balls of baking powder.
3. Add the egg, cream and vanilla extract to another bowl and stir to blend.

4. Pour the wet ingredients into the dry ones and stir until they are homogeneous.
5. Grease the bottom and sides of a microwaveable dish with the butter and pour in the mix.
6. Microwave for 1 minute 20 seconds.
7. Then, soften the almond butter in the oven, pour over the top of the cake and serve.

Orange Chicken with Cranberry Sauce

Ingredients:

- 4 boneless chicken thighs
- A mix of your preferred spices
- Pink salt, sea salt and grounded pepper to taste
- Few tablespoons orange juice and some orange wedges
- Avocado oil or olive oil
- 1 pound of halved brussel sprouts
- 5 oz of fresh cranberries
- 1 tablespoon of Monk fruit sweetener
- The zest of one orange
- Water

Directions:

1. Heat your oven to 375 °F.
2. Dry your chicken thighs and season them with your selection of spices, salt, and pepper to taste.

3. Also add orange juice, a couple orange wedges, and avocado or olive oil.
4. Marinate for at least 30 minutes, the more the better.
5. Add the halved Brussel sprouts to a pan sheet with salt and pepper to taste and a dash of avocado oil.
6. Put both pans in the oven and cook them for 20 minutes.
7. Then, turn the oven to broil or 420 °F and cook them both for an extra 5 minutes.
8. For the cranberry sauce, add the cranberries to a large saucepan.
9. Add the fruit sweetener, the zest, and some water and cook for 20 minutes, until the cranberries pop and it starts to thicken.
10. If it gets too dense, you can add a bit of orange juice or some water.
11. Serve some cranberry sauce on a plate and add the chicken and Brussel sprouts on top.

Loaded Breakfast Muffins

Ingredients:

- 2 small carrots, peeled and grated
- Salt and freshly ground black pepper to taste
- 1 lb. grass-fed ground chicken
- 1 small onion, chopped
- ½ teaspoon oregano, dried and crushed
- 2 small garlic cloves, minced
- 2 tablespoons olive oil, divided
- ½ medium sweet potato, peeled and grated
- 1 cup fresh mushrooms, chopped
- 8 large organic eggs, beaten

Directions:

1. Preheat your oven to 355°Fahrenheit. Lightly grease 12-cup muffin pan.

2. Take large pan and heat 1 tablespoon of oil over medium heat and sauté onion for 5 minutes.
3. Add the garlic and oregano to pan and sauté for 1 minute.
4. Add the chicken, salt, black pepper and cook for 7 minutes.
5. Transfer the chicken mixture into a bowl.
6. Take your remaining oil and add to same pan and cook carrots and sweet potato for 3 minutes.
7. Place mushrooms into pan and cook for another 2 minutes.
8. Stir in some salt and pepper and cook for another 3 minutes.
9. Transfer the vegetable mixture into the bowl with chicken mixture and mix well.
10. Add the beaten eggs and mix well.
11. Add the mixture to prepared muffin tins.

12. Put into your oven and bake for 20 minutes or until they become golden-brown.
13. Remove the muffin tin from oven and keep onto a wire rack to cool for about 10 minutes.
14. Carefully invert the wire rack and serve warm.

Holiday Muffins

Ingredients:

- 2 ½ cups almond flour
- ¼ teaspoon salt
- Pinch of ground cloves
- Pinch of nutmeg
- ½ teaspoon ground cinnamon
- ¾ teaspoon baking soda
- 1 teaspoon apple cider vinegar
- 2 tablespoons organic honey
- 2 tablespoons coconut oil, melted
- 3 large organic eggs

- 1 cup fresh blueberries
- 1/3 cup homemade pumpkin puree
- 1 teaspoon organic vanilla extract

Directions:

1. Preheat the oven to 350°Fahrenheit. Line cups of muffin tin with paper liners.
2. In a mixing bowl, mix baking soda, flour, spices and salt.
3. In another bowl, add coconut oil, eggs, honey, vinegar and vanilla extract and mix well.
4. Add pumpkin puree and beat well to combine.
5. Add the egg mixture to flour mixture and mix well.
6. Gently, fold in blueberries.
7. Place the mixture into prepared muffin cups.
8. Bake for 18 minutes.
9. Remove from your oven and keep on wire rack to cool for about 5 minutes.

10. Carefully, invert the muffins onto wire rack to completely cool before serving.

Carrot Bread

Ingredients:

- 2 cups almond flour
- ½ cup carrot, peeled and shredded
- 1 teaspoon ground cinnamon
- 1 teaspoon baking soda
- 1 teaspoon organic baking powder
- 2 tablespoons coconut flour
- 1/3 cup coconut oil, melted
- 1/3 cup organic honey
- 3 organic eggs
- ¼ teaspoon salt
- ¼ teaspoon salt
- ¼ cup walnuts, chopped

Directions:

1. Preheat the oven to 325°Fahrenheit. Grease a loaf pan.
2. In mixing bowl, add baking soda, baking powder, flour, cinnamon and salt.
3. In another bowl, mix eggs, coconut oil, honey and carrot and mix well.
4. Add the flour mixture with egg mixture and mix well.
5. Gently, fold in the walnuts.
6. Transfer the mixture to prepared loaf pan.
7. Bake for about 38 minutes. Add to a wire rack to allow to cool for 10 minutes.
8. Invert your bread onto wire rack and slice and serve.

Pumpkin Pie

Ingredients:

Pie Crust

- 1 cup pitted dates
- ½ cup oatmeal
- ½ cup pecan nuts

Pumpkin Spice Mixture

- 4 teaspoons cinnamon
- 2 teaspoons allspice
- 2 teaspoons nutmeg
- 1 teaspoon ginger
- 1 teaspoon ground cloves

Pumpkin Filling

- 15 ounces of canned pure pumpkin
- 2/3 cup unsalted cashew nuts
- 1/3 cup cashew milk (or another plant milk such as almond)
- ½ cup maple syrup
- 1 tablespoon orange juice

- Zest of one orange

- 1 tablespoon of pumpkin spice mixture (ingredients shown above)

- 1 tablespoon arrowroot powder

Directions:
1. Pre-heat the oven to 400 degrees Fahrenheit.
2. Put all the pie crust ingredients into a food processor or blender. Process until clumps start to form.
3. With your hands press the pie crust mixture into an 8 x 8 glass ovenproof dish (can be greased with coconut oil), making sure you work it up the sides of the dish.
4. In the food processor or blender process the pumpkin filling ingredients until they are smooth and creamy.
5. Pour the ingredients into your pie crust and bake for 10 minutes.

6. After 10 minutes lower the temperature to 350 degrees Fahrenheit and bake for a further 20 to 25 minutes until golden brown.
7. Allow to cool and then chill in the refrigerator for at least one hour.
8. Serve with coconut cream or almond milk ice-cream.

Spiced Fruit Salad

Ingredients:

- 1 small pineapple
- 1 melon of choice (Honeydew, Cantaloupe, Gallia, Charentais)
- 2 cups fresh strawberries
- 1 cup blueberries
- 1 lime
- 1 teaspoon cinnamon powder
- 1 teaspoon ginger powder
- ½ teaspoon cayenne powder

Directions:

1. Skin the pineapple and cut into 1-inch cubes
2. Skin and deseed the melon and cut into 1-inch cubes
3. Cut strawberries in half

4. Wash the blueberries
5. Place all fruit and spices into a bowl
6. Grate the skin of the lime and add it to the bowl
7. Add the juice of the lime to the bowl
8. Mix gently until combined
9. Refrigerate for 1 hour or longer
10. Enjoy
11. Can be stored in an airtight container in the fridge for up to 3 days providing the strawberries were really fresh.

Vegan Chocolate Mousse

Ingredients:

- 1 can 14 ounces Coconut Cream
- 1 cup pitted Medjol dates
- ¼ cup Cocoa powder

Directions:

1. Place the can of coconut cream in the fridge overnight. When you're ready to make your mousse open it up and scoop out just the hardened cream that you'll find on top.
2. Remove the skin from the dates with a small knife and then push them through a metal sieve
3. Add the sieved dates, cocoa powder and hardened coconut cream to a food processor and process until smooth.
4. Divide between two ramekins before placing in the fridge to set.

5. Can be served with a dollop of whipped coconut cream, vegan chocolate shavings and cherries (optional).

Nests of Sweet Potato Eggs

Ingredients:

- Two big shredded sweet potatoes
- Two tsp olive oil
- One tsp of paprika
- To taste, add salt and pepper.
- Four big eggs
- Freshly chopped chives, optional as a garnish

Directions

1. Turn the oven on to 375°F, or 190°C. Use nonstick cooking spray to grease a muffin pan.

2. Cut up sweet potatoes.
3. Use a box grater to finely shred the sweet potatoes. Squeeze off any extra moisture

from the shredded sweet potatoes by placing them in a fresh kitchen towel.

4. Nest Form and Season
5. Combine the grated sweet potatoes, paprika, olive oil, salt, and pepper in a bowl. Distribute the mixture equally between the muffin tin cups, creating nests by pushing them up against the sides.

6. Cook Nests of Sweet Potatoes
7. Bake for approximately 15 minutes, or until the edges are golden and crispy, in the preheated oven for the sweet potato nests.

8. Bake with eggs added.
9. One egg should be carefully cracked into each sweet potato nest. Place the muffin tray back in the oven and continue baking for a further

12 to 15 minutes, or until the yolks are still somewhat runny but the egg whites are set.

10. Serve and Garnish
11. Serve these Sweet Potato Egg Nests warm, garnished with chopped fresh chives for a pop of freshness.

12. Savour a Nest of Happiness
13. Enter these charming nests and experience the harmony of poached eggs and sweet potatoes. It's a visually appealing and aesthetically pleasant brunch dish.

Tortillas using Cassava Flour

Ingredients

- Two cup of flour made from cassava
- Half a cup of tapioca flour
- 1/4 cup melted coconut oil
- Salt, one teaspoon
- One cup of hot water

Directions

1. Mix the tapioca flour, cassava flour, and salt in a big basin.
2. Pour Wet Ingredients in.
3. Add warm water and melted coconut oil. Stir to make a dough.
4. Rest and Knead

5. After transferring the dough to a surface that has been slightly floured, knead it for a few minutes until it becomes smooth. Give the dough ten minutes or so to rest.

6. Separate and Turn
7. Divide the dough into golf-ball-sized pieces. Form each part into a ball and use your hands to flatten it.

8. Presenting the Tortillas
9. Roll a flattened ball into a thin tortilla by placing it between two pieces of parchment paper. Continue with the leftover dough balls.

10. Use a hob to cook.
11. In a skillet, preheat the heat to medium-high. Every tortilla should be cooked for one to two minutes on each side, or until it puffs up and appears as light brown patches.

12. Keep Warm
13. Serve your Cassava Flour Tortillas warm after stacking them. They are prepared for you to fill them with your Ingredients: to make a delectable supper.

Flapjacks with Cinnamon Cassava Flour

Ingredients:

- Two cups of flour made from cassava
- Two tsp powdered baking
- One teaspoon of cinnamon powder
- One-fourth teaspoon salt
- Two egg
- 1 1/2 cups almond milk (or any other type of milk).
- Two tsp pure maple syrup
- Two teaspoons of coconut oil, melted
- One tsp vanilla essence

Directions:

1. Mix the cassava flour, baking powder, powdered cinnamon, and salt in a big basin.

2. Mix the moist ingredients.
3. Whisk eggs, almond milk, maple syrup, melted coconut oil, and vanilla extract in another dish.

4. Mixture Batter
5. After adding the wet ingredients to the dry, mix just until incorporated. Leave the batter for a few minutes.

6. Cook over a grill.
7. Set a nonstick pan or griddle on medium heat. For each flapjack, pour 1/4 cup of batter onto the griddle.

8. Toss and Prepare
9. Cook until surface bubbles appear, then turn and continue cooking until golden brown on the other side.

10. Present with garnishes.
11. Arrange your Cinnamon Cassava Flour Flapjacks in a stack and top with your preferred toppings, such as yoghurt, fresh fruit, or a maple syrup drizzle.

12. Savour the bliss of cinnamon.
13. Indulge in these cosy and warm flapjacks, where the delightful scent of cinnamon permeates the space and turns breakfast into a festive affair.

Soy Honey Salmon

Ingredients:

- 16oz [450g] Wild Salmon, or Vegan Meat
- 2 cloves Garlic (sliced)
- 1 cup [120mL] Soy Honey Glaze
- 1 Tbsp [15mL] Avocado Oil (or Organic Red Palm, or Extra Virgin Olive Oil)
- 1 Lemon (sliced into wedges, for garnish)

Directions:

1. On a baking sheet, grease it thoroughly with the oil. Add the fish fillet or vegan meat, then thoroughly coat that with the soy honey glaze.
2. Garnish the fish or vegan meat with sliced garlic. You can optionally add the lemon wedges here if you're going to broil it.
3. Broil on High on the top oven rack for 6-8 minutes. Alternatively, you can grill on

medium-high for 3-4 minutes per side.

(Optional) Use a silicon grill mat (not aluminum foil) so the fish doesn't stick to your grill and stink it up.
4. Garnish with lemon wedges (if you didn't broil them). Serve and enjoy!

Spicy Pork (daeji bulgogi)

Ingredients:

- 2 pounds [900g] Pork (Butt, or Loin) or Vegan Meat, or Vegetables

- 1 Onion (minced)

- 2 cloves Garlic (crushed, or minced)

- 1 inch [2.5cm] Ginger (peeled and grated)

- 2 Tbsp [30mL] Gochujang Sauce

- 1 Tbsp [15mL] Sesame Oil

- 1 Tbsp [15mL] Coconut Aminos

- 2 Tbsp [30mL] Swerve, or Sweetener

- 1 Tbsp [15mL] Sake, or Rice Vinegar plus 1 drop Stevia

- 1 tsp [5mL] Iodized Sea Salt

Directions:

1. Slice the pork into very thin pieces, about the thickness of a slice of bacon.
2. Or cut the vegan meat, or vegetables similarly.
3. Add all the ingredients to a large mixing bowl and mix vigorously. Marinate for 30-60 minutes.
4. Grill, broil, or pan fry the meat, vegan meat, or vegetables for 4-8 minutes depending on how quickly it's heating through.
5. The thin slices will make it cook faster, so be mindful of an open flame.
6. Serve and enjoy! This is great along with sides, inside of a lettuce wrap with avocado and kimchi, or on top of rice or noodles.

Spicy Rice Cakes (duk boki)

Ingredients:

- 1 pound [450g] Rice Cakes (duk) or 2 packages Trader Joe's Cauliflower Gnocchi

- 8oz [230g] Fish Cake (leftover, or fresh – vegan sub Mushrooms)

- 2 cups [450g] Napa Cabbage (chopped)

- 3 Shiitake Mushrooms (sliced)

- 2 cloves Garlic (crushed, or minced)

- 1-3 cups [250-750mL] Water

- 2 Tbsp [30mL] Sweet Potato Starch, or Tapioca Starch

- 1 ½ Tbsp [25mL] Coconut Aminos

- 1 Tbsp [15mL] Swerve, or Sweetener

- 1 Tbsp [15mL] Gochujang Sauce

- 1 tsp [5mL] Iodized Sea Salt
- 1 tsp [5mL] Cayenne Pepper (or Black Pepper if avoiding nightshades)

Directions:

1. If using actual rice cake (*duk*) then soak it for an hour in cold water. If you're using Trader Joe's gnocchi, just open the bags and you're set.
2. In a large pot, add the gochujang, cayenne or black pepper, garlic, swerve or sweetener, and coconut aminos. If you're using actual rice cake, add 3 cups [720mL] of water. If you're using TJ gnocchi, add 1 cup [240mL] water. Bring it to a boil.
3. Add the vegetables and rice cakes, or gnocchi, and fish cakes. Simmer for 10 minutes. The

sauce should continue to thicken, even with the heat off.
4. Serve, and enjoy!

ENERGIZING DAILY TONIC

Ingredients:

- 2-4 tbsp vegan protein powder.

- 1 tbsp maca powder.

- 1 tsp ashwagandha powder.

- 1 tsp mushroom blend powder.

- 1 tsp astragalus powder.

- 1/4 cup pecans.

- 2 Brazil nuts.

- If you desire it really velvety), 2 cups hot water (or nondairy milk.

- Pinch of stevia powder.

- 1-2 tbsp maple syrup or dates

- 1 tbsp cacao powder.

- 1 tbsp ground coffee.

- 1/2 tsp vanilla extract.

- 1/2 tsp apple pie spice mix, as desired.

Direction:

1. Blend all the base active ingredients except the maple syrup up until smooth, velvety and tasty.
2. Include 1 to 2 tablespoons of maple syrup or a small handful of dates, if you desire it sweeter.
3. It is suggested to mix in the add-ons if you are using a plain protein powder.
4. The protein powder this dish utilized currently has coffee and chocolate in it, so it supplies a great deal of tasty flavor. Don't utilize a gross-tasting protein powder!
5. Sprinkle with apple pie spice, if utilizing, and enjoy!

STRAWBERRY MAPLE SCONES

Ingredients:

- 2 cups oat flour.

- 1/3 cup almond milk.

- 1 cup of strawberries.

- A handful of dried currants.

- 5 tbsp coconut oil.

- 5 tbsp of maple syrup.

- 1 tbsp baking powder.

- 1 1/2 tsp vanilla extract.

- 1 tsp cinnamon.

- 1/2 tsp cardamom (optional).

- Sprinkle of salt.

Directions:

1. Include the coconut oil and with a pastry cutter or fork, cut and blend the coconut oil

into the oat flour mix until a crumbly dough forms.
2. As soon as it is cold, add the strawberry pieces, currants and slowly include in all the wet ingredients.
3. Slowly blend the dry and wet components until combined - mindful not to over mix.
4. On a baking sheet lined with parchment paper, form a circle out of the dough - it must have to do with 1 inch thick. Cut into eight triangular pieces and bake for 15-17 minutes. Delight in with jam, a drizzle of honey or nut butter!

HIGH-PROTEIN VANILLA AND CASHEW SMOOTHIE

Ingredients:

- 2 frozen bananas.
- 1 and 1/2 cups almond milk.
- 1 tbsp cashew butter.
- 1 scoop protein powder.
- 1 tbsp maca powder.

Directions:

1. Merely blend whatever into a high-speed blender and mix till smooth and creamy.

SPINACH TOFU SCRAMBLE WITH SOUR CREAM

Ingredients:

Sour cream:

- 75 g raw cashews, soaked overnight,
- 30 ml lemon juice,
- 5 g nutritional yeast,
- 60 ml water 1 good pinch salt,
- 15 ml olive oil.
- 1 small onion, diced.
- 1 clove garlic, minced.
- 400 firm tofu, pressed, crumbled.
- 1/2 tsp ground cumin.
- 1/2 tsp curry powder.
- 1/2 tsp turmeric.
- 2 tomatoes, diced.

- 30 g baby spinach

- Salt, to taste.

Directions:

1. Make the cashew sour cream; rinse and drain soaked cashews.
2. Place the cashews, lemon juice, nutritional yeast, water, and salt in a food processor.
3. Blend on high until smooth, for 5-6 minutes.
4. Transfer to a bowl and place aside. Make the tofu scramble; heat olive oil in a skillet.
5. Add onion and cook 5 minutes over medium-high.
6. Add garlic, and cook stirring, for 1 minute.
7. Add crumbled tofu and stir to coat with oil.
8. Add the cumin, curry, and turmeric. Cook the tofu for 2 minutes.
9. Add the tomatoes and cook for 2 minutes.
10. Add spinach and cook, tossing until completely wilted, about 1 minute. Transfer tofu scramble on the plate.

11. Top with a sour cream and serve.

www.ingramcontent.com/pod-product-compliance
Lightning Source LLC
LaVergne TN
LVHW010222070526
838199LV00062B/4695